Kamalika's Recipes with Love

Recipes, flavours and cooking tips using natural spices to add a modern twist to any dish

Kamalika Ranasingha

Copyright © Kamalika Ranasingha, 2021.

978-1-914225-58-1

All rights reserved.

No part of this book may be copied, reproduced, stored or transmitted in any way, including any written, electronic, recording, or photocopying without written permission of the author and publisher. Although every precaution has been taken to verify the accuracy of the information contained herein, the author and publisher assume no responsibility for any errors or omissions. The rights for images used remain with the originator. Also, note that the cooking efforts and recipes may turn out different from those shown in the photographs. They are presented for demonstration purposes only.

Published in Ireland by Orla Kelly Publishing.

INTRODUCTION TO THE BOOK

This book celebrates love and the importance of having wonderful people in my life to fulfill my hopes and dreams. Publishing this book of some of my favourite and much-loved recipes has been a dream come true for me.

I want to mention my husband Dayantha, who has always enjoyed all my dishes and who has taken all the food photographs. This amazing, encouraging person has been with me all the way, and without his support, these dreams would not have been possible. Dayantha is also a great chef, and between us, we have won over 20 culinary awards from around the world.

Let me tell you a bit about myself. I was born on a magnificent island called Sri Lanka, and from a young age, I was certain I would be a chef as all I did was cook.

I was blessed to have a very kind and patient grandmother as all these cooking sessions happened in my grandma's kitchen under her watchful eye. My mind often wanders back to that kitchen, and the smells, tastes, and aroma still tantalise my taste buds. My grandma had the time and patience to encourage me when things went pear-shaped, so I learned to persevere and develop my cooking skills.

I also had my mum's bakery where I improved the skills I had picked up.

These experiences and travelling through many countries developed my food knowledge and creativity.

We arrived in Ireland in 2002 and felt very welcome here, so I want to thank all the chefs, owners, managers, and staff in the fantastic establishments we worked in over the years.

I am so proud of my cookery school, Multifarnham Cookery School that we started in 2012, and it has won Best Cookery School of the Year twice!

As much as I always wanted to write a book, it was more important that it be a book filled with love and meaning in my journey.

Also, I want to thank my wonderful parents, sisters, and friends who have always encouraged my dreams.

Kamalika Ranasingha

Thank you to Adrian for always capturing the perfect pictures of myself and Rachel Penrose for making me look beautiful every time I need her help. Thank you to all the directors and staff at Larcc cancer retreat centre.

CONTENTS

Sri Lankan tuna rolls 1

Seafood tian with Pineapple salsa 4

Prawn balls with roasted sesame seeds 7

Paneer with Tomato and Apricot Chutney 9

Scallops with curried parsnips and pomegranate 11

Tempura battered tiger prawns and coriander 13

Gin, Tonic and lemon marination for chicken wings 15

Arancini with chorizo and tomato sauce 16

Pineapple and date pickle 18

Salsa Fresca 19

Chicken and black pudding roulade 20

Courgette and almond buns 22

Blinis with smoked salmon and beetroot puree 25

Crab souffle with gruyere cheese 27

Coconut Roti 29

Mulinelli del po 33

Salmon with beetroot and wild mushrooms 39

Whole seabream in hot sauce 41

Roasted Greek style lemon chicken 43

Traditional fish curry 49

Tuscan fish stew with fresh fennel salad 51

Venison with Dark Chocolate and red Pepper sauce 53

Oven baked chicken curry 55

Roasted pork loin with pineapple puree and roasted cashew nuts 57

Chicken pilaf 59

Mint sambol 61

Seabass fillets with aubergine and green beans 63

Slow Roasted Lamb Leg with Harissa Paste 65

Monkfish, rosemary & bacon skewers 67

Lentil curry 68

Baked mackerel with pine nuts and chickpea stuffing 70

Steak fillets with red wine jus and sautéed kale 72

Crab meat, anchovies and linguine 74

Roasted butternut squash and butter bean burgers 76

Prawns in coconut milk 78

Coconut salad (sambal) 81

Lamb rack with parsley puree and red cabbage 83

Fish masala 85

Roast duck with potato pancake and spinach 87

Steam fish with ginger 91

Basic curry powder blend 95

SRI LANKAN TUNA ROLLS

This is for my dear mother, who was indeed a very inspiring person in my life. Every time I am fed up and wants to give up, I think of her. She never gave up on whatever life sent her way but kept going. Thanks to her, my two sisters and I grew up seeing this, which made us who we are today.

It gave me the confidence that if you put your heart and soul into anything, it can be achieved.

Also, my mother was a very strict and no-nonsense person, so I learnt a lot from her in the kitchen, but it was not like in my grandmother's kitchen because my mum operated a bakery and restaurant as a business. Working in her kitchen was the best way of practical learning.

This recipe is dedicated to her. She would make at least 200 of these with different fillings. They were so popular that people came from all over Sri Lanka and from all walks of life to taste them.

Whenever she visits us, we always ask her to make these.

Serves 6 to 8

Ingredients

For the pancakes
500g plain flour
1tsp sugar
2tsp salt
1litre milk

100g melted butter
2 eggs

For the tuna filling
200g cooked mash potato
300g cooked tuna
100g grated carrots
2 cloves of garlic
20g grated ginger
4tbsp olive oil
100g chopped onions
1 green chilli deseeded and chopped
½tsp turmeric
Pepper and salt to taste.
10 curry leaves (optional)

Batter for coating
500g bread crumbs
100g plain flour
½ litre water

Method
For the pancakes
First the pancakes must be made.
Melt the butter, then add all the other ingredients for the pancake mixture into a large bowl and mix well to a pancake consistency. Finally, add the melted butter.
Heat a non-stick pan and make the pancakes as thin as possible.

For the tuna mixture
Remember, if you are not fond of tuna, use any meat or fish filling, but it must be cooked first.
Add the olive oil to a large pan, then add the onions, garlic and curry leaves and sauté till the onions are golden in colour.
Add the rest of the ingredients, then season with pepper and salt and mix well.
When cooking fresh tuna, make sure to wash it at least once. Then add some lemon juice, crushed black pepper, salt and a little bit of turmeric.
Preheat the oven for 10 minutes at 170°C.
Cover with foil and bake for a further 20 minutes.

Mix the plain flour and water in a large bowl. This is for coating the rolls before they are covered with the bread crumbs.

To assemble
Lay the pancake on a work surface and add a little bit of the tuna mix.
Then roll it quite firmly.
Dip it in the batter and then roll onto the bread crumbs.
Keep repeating.
Once ready, heat some oil in a frying pan and deep fat fry them.

SEAFOOD TIAN WITH PINEAPPLE SALSA

Serves 6

Ingredients
200g smoked mackerel
200g cooked prawns
200g smoked salmon
1 red chilli deseeded and chopped
1tablsp lemon juice
100g cream cheese
50g fresh dill or chives

Method
Place smoked mackerel, smoked salmon, cooked prawns (keep few prawns separate for the garnish), deseeded chilli, cream cheese and fresh dill in a food processor. Mix well to a coarse finish.

Then take a pastry ring approximately 4 inches in width and layer it with the fish mix. Press well. Add the salsa once everything is assembled, and carefully take the pastry ring away. You can also do this in a ramekin.

Notes
Ensure all skin and bones have been removed from the fish. Prawns must be peeled and cooked, or buy them already cooked.

Pineapple & coriander salsa
Ingredients
1 fresh pineapple
1 shallot
1 red pepper
juice of 1 lemon
6 cherry tomatoes
1 tbsp. olive oil
handful of coriander
salt to taste

Method
Peel and dice the pineapple, separating it from the hard centre.
Deseed the pepper and dice.
Chop the shallot and the cherry tomatoes.
Next, place all the ingredients in a large bowl. Add the chopped coriander and mix well.

Notes
Peel and chop the shallots finely and cut cherry tomatoes into small pieces. Dice the pepper into smaller dices. Remove the seeds

PRAWN BALLS WITH ROASTED SESAME SEEDS

Serves 6

Ingredients
250g peeled raw prawns
1 deseeded chilli
3tblsp roasted sesame seeds
2tsp chopped ginger
1 clove garlic
4 spring onions
120g self-raising flour
1 egg
½ tsp fish sauce
500 ml Sunflower oil for deep frying

Method
Wash the spring onions, and cut them into smaller pieces. Next add them along with the ginger, chill, garlic fish sauce and prawns to a food processor.
Process until finely chopped.
Scrape the mixture into a large bowl, then add the flour and sesame seeds.
Whisk the egg lightly and add to the mixture. Season with salt.
Heat the oil in heavy-based saucepan or wok.
Meanwhile, shape a tablespoon full of the prawn mixture into small balls.

Fry the prawn balls in smaller batches for 2 to 3 minutes till golden brown.
Remove with a slotted spoon and drain on kitchen paper.
Arrange on a platter and serve with tomato and apricot chutney if desired.

PANEER WITH TOMATO AND APRICOT CHUTNEY

Serves 6

Ingredients
500g paneer
4tbsp oil

For the marination
2tbsp yoghurt
2 cloves garlic
1tsp ginger
1tsp chilli powder
1tsp gram masala
2tsp salt

Method
Slice the paneer thinly, draining off any liquid.
Chop the garlic and ginger finely, then place all ingredients in a large bowl and mix well.
Next, add the paneer and coat well. If possible, do the marination 4 hours prior.
Heat a pan with the oil and fry the paneer till golden brown.
Arrange in a platter and serve with the tomato chutney.

Tomato and apricot chutney

1kg tomatoes skinned and diced
100g dried apricots chopped
100ml apple cider vinegar
100g sugar
1tsp nutmeg powder
3tsp dried chilli flakes
2 cloves garlic
2tsp salt

Method

Place the tomatoes in a large bowl and add boiling water. After 3 minutes, drain the water.
Remove the skins and dice the tomato.
Place the vinegar, garlic and chilli flakes in a food processor and blend till the garlic is pureed to a smooth texture.
Put the tomatoes, apricots, nutmeg powder, sugar, salt and paste in a heavy-based saucepan.
Simmer on medium heat for about 30 minutes till it attains a thick consistency.

Note: If you would like to keep it for few weeks, sterilise a jar and a lid and pour in the mixture while still hot.
Once cooled, put on the lid and store in the fridge.

SCALLOPS WITH CURRIED PARSNIPS AND POMEGRANATE

Serves 6

Ingredients
12 scallops
200g parsnips
1tsp curry powder
1tsp turmeric
100ml fresh cream
50g butter
2tbs oil
1 pomegranate
1 lime
Sea salt and pepper to taste

Method
Peel and wash the parsnips and place them in a saucepan. Cover with water.
Add in the curry powder, turmeric, and salt and cook.
Once the parsnips are cooked, drain all the water and put them in a food processor along with the cream and butter. Puree to a smooth consistency.

Cut open the pomegranate and remove all seeds and keep it to the side.
Marinate the scallops with the lime juice, pepper, and sea salt.

Heat the oil in a pan and cook six scallops at a time.
Leave each side of the scallop to colour for about 4 minutes before turning over.
Do not cook for more than 8 minutes.
Before serving, first, add about two tablespoons of the parsnip puree with the scallops on top.
Scatter the pomegranate seeds over the dish.

TEMPURA BATTERED TIGER PRAWNS AND CORIANDER

Serves 6

Ingredients
300g self-rising flour
50g cornflour
3 large eggs
1tsp salt
400ml ice cold water
12 tiger prawns peeled and deveined.
1tsp crushed black pepper.
1tsp sea salt
Juice and zest of 1 lime
50g coriander sprigs
100g plain flour
500ml oil for frying

Method
Add all the dry ingredients to a large bowl.
Break the eggs in a separate bowl and whisk them before adding them to the dry Ingredients
Add the water gradually, mixing slowly, being careful not over mix.

Note: The reason for using ice water is when the batter is cold, it helps to cling to the surface of the item being cooked.

The finished batter should be similar to fresh cream consistency. When peeling the prawns, keep the tails on them, then season with lime juice, zest, pepper, and sea salt. Roll in plain flour before dipping in the batter. Do the same with the coriander sprigs.

Heat the oil in a deep fat fryer or a large heavy-based saucepan or wok until the temperature reaches 180°C or until a piece of bread browns in 40 seconds.
Fry only five or six pieces at a time for 4 to 5 minutes till golden brown and crisp. Remove with a slotted spoon. Drain as much oil as possible and leave them on a plate layered with kitchen paper to drain any remaining oil.
If too many pieces are added together to the oil, the oil temperature will drop, and the batter would be soggy after cooking.
Serve with Shoyu as a dipping sauce.

GIN, TONIC AND LEMON MARINATION FOR CHICKEN WINGS

Serves 6 to 8

Ingredients
100ml Dry gin
50ml Tonic water
2teasp Harissa powder
Juice of 3 lemons
Pepper and salt to taste
1kg Chicken wings (only drumettes)
2 lemons cut into wedges for garnish

Method
Mix all ingredients in a large bowl and use this to marinate the wings. Do this the night before serving and leave it in the fridge. Preheat the oven for 10 minutes at 170°C before baking them for a further 25 minutes.
Serve with lemon wedges.

ARANCINI WITH CHORIZO AND TOMATO SAUCE

Serves 6

Ingredients
50g butter
2 tbsp olive oil
200g risotto rice
100g grated parmesan
200g chopped mushrooms
100ml white wine
2 tbsp chopped onion
1litre vegetable stock
100ml fresh cream
1-litre sunflower oil

For coating
2 egg whites
200g breadcrumbs

Method
Heat a large pan with olive oil before adding the butter and chopped mushrooms (preferably the chanterelle variety). If not, chestnut mushrooms are fine. Add an onion and sauté well. Add the risotto rice and cook until the rice is transparent. Add the white wine, and when the wine is absorbed completely, add

200ml of stock. When absorbed, keep adding more in batches till the rice is completely cooked.
Mix in the grated parmesan.
Spread the risotto on a tray and leave it to cool. Once cooled, shape the mixture into bite-size balls.
Whisk the egg whites lightly and dip in the balls followed by coating them with breadcrumbs.
Heat the oil in a large wok and deep fat fry till the outside crumbs are golden brown.

Chorizo and tomato sauce

2tbsp oil
100g chopped chorizo
400g tin chopped tomato
2 cloves garlic
2tsp paprika
100g fresh basil
Pepper and salt to taste

Method

Heat a pan and add the oil, garlic and chorizo. When sautéed, pour in the chopped tomato followed by paprika. Allow the sauce to boil. Finally add the basil and put the sauce in a food processor, blending till smooth. Pour some of the sauce onto a plate, then place the balls on top.

PINEAPPLE AND DATE PICKLE

Serves 6

Ingredients
200g chopped dates
100g sultanas
3tsp wholegrain mustard
600g fresh pineapple chunks
3tsp chilli flakes
100ml white vinegar
10 peeled shallots
2tsp salt

Method
Make sure the dates are deseeded.
Peel the pineapple and dice, taking out the hard core.
Mix all ingredients in a pan and bring it to a boil. Then simmer for 30 minutes.
When cool, store in a sterilised glass jar.

SALSA FRESCA

Serves 6

Ingredients

200g chopped tomatoes
50g sundried tomatoes
Juice of 1 lime
Handful of fresh parsley
2 garlic cloves crushed
2tbs olive oil
1 bunch of scallions sliced
1tsp salt
1tbsp tomato puree
1 diced pepper
20ml beer

Method

Mix the olive oil, tomato puree and beer in a large bowl before adding the rest of the ingredients to the mixture.
Leave the salsa to stand for at least one hour before serving.

CHICKEN AND BLACK PUDDING ROULADE

Serves 6

Ingredients
400g chicken breast
2tbsp chopped parsley
100g black pudding
2tsp harissa powder
Salt and pepper to taste
100g dried cranberry
1 large onion diced finely

2 pieces of 10-inch foil and the same size cling film for wrapping

Method
Dice the chicken and place in a food processor with the diced onion and blend until the chicken has a smooth paste texture.
Add in the parsley and seasoning and blend again for 1 minute.
Dice the black pudding into small squares, add some oil, and panfry the black pudding, being careful not to break it up.
Once the black pudding cools down, mix it gently with the chicken mix using a spatula. Next add in the cranberry.
Weigh and divide the mixture into equal portions.
Cut a large piece of foil and the same size of cling film, approximately 10-inch square.

Place the mixture on the cling film and tightly wrap the cling film to form a sausage shape "roulade" with the mixture evenly distributed with no air bubbles.
Place the roulade over a steamer and cover with a lid. Make sure that when steaming, moisture cannot get in. Cover with foil.

Wait till steam starts to generate, and time 25 minutes or if using a temperature probe, the core temperature should be 75°C or over.
Serve cold or warm with salsa.

COURGETTE AND ALMOND BUNS

Serves 6

Ingredients
400g grated courgette
250g almond powder
100g grated mozzerella
2 cloves chopped garlic
4 large eggs
2tsp curry powder
150g melted butter
1tsp salt
(can add grated carrots)

Method
Add the grated courgette, almond powder, curry powder, salt, mozzarella and garlic to a large bowl and mix.
Break the eggs into a separate container and whisk.
Melt the butter in a pan.
Add the eggs first to the dry ingredients, and then add the butter. Mix well.
Add cupcake cases to a bun mould and divide the mixture into 12 equal portions.

Preheat the oven at 170°C for 10 minutes and bake for a further 15 minutes.

NOTES

BLINIS WITH SMOKED SALMON AND BEETROOT PUREE

Serves 6 to 8

Ingredients
For the blinis
100g plain flour
1 egg
150ml milk
40g butter
Handful of chives
Season with salt

Method
Place the flour in a large bowl and season with salt.
Make a well in the centre and add the egg.
Melt the butter in a separate pan.
Whisk in the milk gradually, and then add the melted butter before mixing well.
Fold in the chopped chives.
To cook lightly, grease a frying pan. Then add a tablespoon full of the mix. Three can be made at a time in a small pan keep them apart.
Cook for 2 minutes on each side until golden in colour.

Beetroot puree

Ingredients
200g cooked and peeled beetroot
100g cream cheese
Pepper and salt to taste
200g smoked salmon

Method
Place the beetroot and cream cheese in a food processor and season with pepper and salt.
Then blend till smooth.

When blinis are cold, assemble them in a platter. Scoop some beetroot on top, followed by the smoked salmon garnish with chives.

CRAB SOUFFLE WITH GRUYERE CHEESE

Serves 6

Ingredients
50g breadcrumbs
450g fresh crabmeat
2 cloves garlic
4tsp mustard powder
50g plain flour
450ml milk
100g gruyere cheese
6 eggs separated
2tsp cayenne pepper
4tbsp fresh chopped chives

Method
Preheat the oven to 200°C for 10 minutes.
Generously grease six individual souffle dishes. Depending on the size of the dishes, if there is any extra mix remaining, have few more moulds ready.
Melt the butter in a large saucepan and add the garlic. When the garlic is cooked, mix in the mustard and flour and continue stirring for a few minutes.
Then gradually pour in the milk while stirring constantly. Bring the mix to a boil.

Remove from the heat and stir in the cheese. Leave the mix to cool.

Lightly beat the egg yolks, then fold in the crabmeat, chives, cayenne pepper and salt to taste.

Whisk the egg whites in a clean bowl until they hold stiff peaks.

Add a large spoonful of the egg white to the crab mixture and fold together.

Keep adding all the remaining egg white.

Spoon onto the prepared dishes.

Cook in the preheated oven for 20 minutes till well risen and golden.

Serve straight away.

COCONUT ROTI

Serves 6

Ingredients
250g grated fresh coconut
400g self-rising flour
100g soft butter
2tsp salt
¼ lit cold water
2 grated carrots
1 finely chopped white onion.
1 deseeded green chilli (optional)

Method
Add all dry ingredients to a large bowl and mix well.
If using green chilli, deseed and chop finely. Mix with the dry ingredients.
Peel and dice the onion finely.
Peel and grate the carrots.
Then gradually add the water. Mix to a soft bread dough consistency.
Add some oil to a work surface and divide the dough into ten equal portions.
Then flatten them with the fingers like mini pizzas.
Heat a pan and add oil. Add the flattened dough onto the pan and cook on low heat for about 8 minutes on one side, then turn over and cook the other side for about 5 minutes till both sides are golden brown in colour.

Tip
If using desiccated coconut, we must hydrate it before use since it is dehydrated. To do this, warm 100ml of coconut milk and pour onto the desiccated coconut and set aside for about 5 minutes before mixing with the other ingredients.
You will need less water when using desiccated coconut.
If freshly grated coconut is unavailable, desiccated coconut can be used. However, desiccated coconut is sweeter so extra chilli might be needed.

NOTES

MULINELLI DEL PO

The meaning of this dish is Whirlpools of the Po river in Italy because when you cut and place the pasta in a dish, it looks like whirlpools or a swiss roll effect.

So where and how can I even start to describe this wonderful person Battista Ottolini?

I was so lucky to meet him and have him in my life for nearly sixteen years.

This wonderful dish is his creation, and it was made at Christmas time for all his friends as a gift.

I was his assistant at the time, and we always had so much fun making these.

I am so glad that he gave me such perfect recipes and time to master this dish.

He was a very talented chef who started his career in Switzerland around World War Two at the bottom of the kitchen rank and worked to be a MasterChef. He was able to speak more than six languages.

In a nutshell, Battista was a dad, and a friend combined whom we often asked for advice.

We miss him so much. His witty sense of humour, delicious food always freshly made for us, and we look back with treasured memories of the good times and thank him for being there and for the guidance given.

Serves 6

Ingredients

For the white sauce
500ml fresh milk
500ml fresh cream
100g butter
50g plain flour
4tbsp olive oil
1tsp bouillon powder
Pepper and salt
500g cooked slice ham
200g parmesan cheese grated finely
100ml fresh cream (for the final dish for baking)

Method

In a large saucepan, melt the butter along with the olive oil.

When the butter is melted, add the flour and mix well with a spoon. This is called a roux.

Then add the cream and milk which had been mixed together in a jug, and start pouring this into the roux. Ensure that when making this sauce, it needs to be whisked thoroughly until thick. Take the sauce off the heat and season to your preference.

Traditionally it was made with ham, but smoked salmon can be used too.

Cut the ham into small dices, so it is easy to roll the pasta.

Ingredients

For the fresh pasta
500g pasta flour or 00flour
5 eggs
1tsp salt
50ml water

Method

This dough can be kneaded by hand or an electric mixer using the dough hook.

Place all ingredients in a bowl except the water and mix well.

If it is not coming together, then add some of the water, being extremely careful not to make the dough too soft.

Once the dough is made, it must be left to rest in the fridge for at least five hours before being used.

Start with small portions of the dough, putting it through the pasta machine, from the highest number and gradually reducing.

Always keep dusting with flour so that it does not get stuck in the machine.

The sheets should be the same thickness as a lasagne sheet.

For this recipe, about six sheets are needed.

Add water to a large saucepan with a pinch of salt and when the water comes to a boil, drop in one pasta sheet at a time and cook the sheets for 5 minutes.

After this time, immediately drop into cold water.

Arrange the pasta sheets on a work surface and very carefully spread the white sauce with a pallet knife on every sheet.

Then scatter the chopped ham, sprinkle the grated parmesan and roll nice and tightly. Let it rest for 30 minutes.

Cut each roll into a thickness of ½ inch.

Preheat the oven for 10 minutes at 170°C.

Add about 100ml fresh cream to an oven dish and arrange the pasta facing up.

Scatter the grated parmesan on top of the pasta and bake for a further 15 minutes.

NOTES

SALMON WITH BEETROOT AND WILD MUSHROOMS

Serves 6

Ingredients
6 salmon fillets (150g each)
2tblsp olive oil
4tsp lemon pepper
Juice and zest of one orange
2 large beetroot (200g)
200g wild mushrooms
1 white onion sliced
2 cloves garlic
3tblsp balsamic vinegar
200ml white wine
Segments of two oranges for the garnish

Method
Wash and clean the salmon fillet making sure there are no bones.
Place it in a glass bowl and add the orange zest, juice, salt to taste and the lemon pepper.
Heat a large pan and pour in the oil. When the oil is well heated, place the skin side of the salmon on the pan to crispen.
Then turn over and pour on the white wine.
Reduce the temperature and let it cook for about 15 to 20 minutes, depending on the size and thickness of the fish.

Precook the beetroot by wrapping them in foil and bake in a preheated oven at 170°C for about 40 minutes, making sure not to overcook. Once cooked, peel and dice quite finely.

Peel the oranges used for the garnish and separate the segments. Heat a pan, add a tiny bit of oil, then add the chopped garlic and sliced onion. Cut the wild mushrooms quite big and add to the pan. Sauté till the mushrooms are cooked, and the onions are sautéed.

Mix in the diced beetroot with the mushrooms and pour on the balsamic vinegar.

Finally, add salt and pepper to taste before bringing the sauce to a boil.

Serve the salmon on a bed of mushroom and beetroot with fresh segments of orange as the garnish.

WHOLE SEABREAM IN HOT SAUCE

Serves 6

Ingredients
3 seabreams
4tbs soya sauce
2tbs rice vinegar
Juice of a lemon
Salt and pepper
100g plain flour for dusting the fish before frying.

For the sauce
4tbs rice vinegar
3tbs soya sauce
2tsp sesame oil
4tbs fish sauce
100ml water
2tsp cornflour
2 sticks of celery
2tbs chopped ginger
4 cloves garlic
4 deseeded chopped chillies

Method
Prepare the fish by descaling and removing any insides.
Rinse the fish inside and out under cold running water before patting dry with kitchen paper.
Using a sharp knife, make series of diagonal slashes on both sides of the fish.
Put into a large glass or nonmetal bowl.
Pour in the soya sauce, rice vinegar, lemon juice, salt, and pepper.
Rub the mix on the fish and leave to marinate at least for three hours or, if time permitting, overnight in the fridge.

For the sauce
Heat the sesame oil in a large pan.
Add in the garlic, ginger, celery and chillies, cook till the garlic is sautéed.
Pour in the fish sauce, rice vinegar and soya sauce. Bring the sauce to a boil and reduce the temperature to a low setting.
Dilute the cornflour in the cold water and pour into the sauce. Keep stirring till a nice thickness is acquired.

For cooking the fish
Heat enough oil in a pan to cover the fish. Dust the fish with flour.
Fry the fish for 15 minutes, turning it over till the fish is crisp. (If cooking in the oven, preheat the oven at 170°C for 10 minutes and bake for a further 20 minutes. For whole fish fillets, cook for 15 minutes.
Arrange the fish on a large platter and pour the sauce on top.

If you dislike using a whole fish, fillets can be used. The cooking time will differ. It can also be oven-baked.

ROASTED GREEK STYLE LEMON CHICKEN

Serves 6 to 8

Ingredients
6 chicken thighs or breast
10 cloves of garlic
4tbsp honey
3tsp oregano
4tsp paprika
6 lemons
2tsp crushed black pepper
4tblsp olive oil
Sprig of rosemary
Handful of chopped parsley
Sea salt to taste

Method
If possible, do this marination the evening before for a better flavour profile.
Slice three lemons the other three zest and juice.
Preheat the oven at 170°C for10 minutes.
Place the chicken thighs in a large bowl.
Then mix all the other ingredients in another bowl. (Do not mix the parsley).
Pour the marination mix on the chicken and arrange the chicken pieces in an oven dish. Add the sliced lemons on top.
Bake for 45 minutes in the preheated oven.
Just before serving, add the chopped parsley on top.

Kamalika Ranasingha

TRADITIONAL FISH CURRY

If anyone ever asked where the inspiration for cooking came, it wasn't from watching any famous chefs; it was from working in my grandmother's kitchen.

My grandma had all the patience in the world, and she let me do all things without any restrictions. I grew up admiring and watching what she does and followed the exact steps.

My first few dishes weren't perfect, but my grandparents and my parents always tasted and gave constructive feedback on areas to improve. I still use so many of my grandma's beautiful recipes. Here is one of them.

So, thank you for that love and guidance given to me.

Serves 6

Ingredients

1kg of sword fish diced
1 large onion diced
50g chopped garlic
100g fresh tomatoes diced
10 curry leaves
10g mustard seeds
2tbsp curry powder
1tsp chilli powder
2tsp turmeric powder
1tsp crushed black pepper
1tbsp tamarind paste

400ml coconut milk
1tsp coconut oil
Salt to taste

Method

We always did this beautiful recipe in a large clay pot on an open fire back home, but a pan works fine too.
Heat a large pan with the coconut oil, then add the mustard seeds. When the mustard seeds start to splatter, add the onions, garlic, curry leaves, curry powder, chilli powder and turmeric powder. Mix very well.
Then add the fish tamarind paste, pepper, salt and tomato.
Lower the heating to a minimum, add half of the coconut milk, cover with a lid and let it cook for 10 minutes.
According to my grandma, the key to cooking the fish curry is not to stir because the fish would break, so just gently shake the pot.
Then add the other half of the coconut milk and cook gently on low heat for about 10 minutes.
Let it rest for at least 10 minutes before serving.

TUSCAN FISH STEW WITH FRESH FENNEL SALAD

Serves 6

Ingredients
1 stick of celery
4 shallots
2 cloves garlic
100ml white wine
2tsp dried chilli flakes
2tsp fennel seeds
12 large peeled fresh prawns
200g monkfish tails
200g mussels
2tblsp olive oil
200ml passata
100ml fish or vegetable stock
Sprig of rosemary
Juice of 1 lemon
For the salad:
1 fennel bulb
2tbsp olive oil
1tbsp red wine vinegar
Handful of chopped parsley
Sea salt

To serve
Garlic bread or crusty rolls

Method

Wash and dice the celery. Peel and finely chop the shallots and garlic.
Cut the monkfish tails into four pieces or for a large tail, cut into six pieces.
Clean the mussels by scrubbing the shells and pulling out any beards that are attached to them. Discard any broken and opened ones.
Heat a heavy-based pan with olive oil, and then add the celery, shallots, and garlic.
Sauté them for a while, then add fennel seeds and chilli flakes.
Next, add the white wine, a rosemary sprig, and fish stock and reduce for 5 minutes.
Mix in the passata, then add the monkfish. Cover with a lid and let it cook for 15 minutes at medium to low temperature.
Take the lid off and add the prawns and cook for 3 minutes.
Then add the mussels and cover with the lid and cook for a further 5 minutes till the shells open. If any shells are not opened, discard them.
Finally, add the lemon juice.

For the salad
Shred the fennel finely. Mix the vinegar and olive oil together in a separate bowl. Then mix everything together. Serve on the side with the stew and bread.

VENISON WITH DARK CHOCOLATE AND RED PEPPER SAUCE

Serves 6

Ingredients
1kg venison loin
100g butter
50ml olive oil
Pepper and salt to taste
For the sauce
6 shallots
6 cloves garlic
350ml red wine
350ml vegetable stock
200g dark chocolate (good quality 70% cocoa)
2tblsp crushed red pepper.
100g pancetta
3 sprigs thyme
6 bay leaves

Method
Heat the pan with oil. Season the meat with one tablespoon of red pepper, then seal the meat.
Add in the butter and baste the meat for a few minutes.
Wrap the meat and place it in a preheated oven at 170°C for 20 minutes.

For the sauce
Use the same pan used for the meat. Add shallots, pancetta, garlic, bay leaves, and thyme. Sauté well. Add the wine and reduce followed by the stock and further reduction. Next strain all the bits and add the remaining red pepper. Bring the sauce back to a boil and turn off the heat. Break the chocolate into small pieces and add to the sauce stirring all the time. If the sauce tends to curdle, change pots straight away.

Slice the venison into thin slices and drizzle the sauce on top.

OVEN BAKED CHICKEN CURRY

Serves 6

Ingredients
6 pieces of chicken thighs or chicken breast
400ml coconut milk
1 white onion diced
1 red pepper
2tblsp chopped ginger.
1 stick of lemongrass
2 deseeded chillies
2tsp turmeric powder
1tsp chilli powder
1tsp black pepper
6 cloves of garlic
3tsp mild curry powder
2 potato's peeled and diced.
4 carrots cut into large pieces.
Sea salt to taste

Method
Preheat the oven at 170°C for 10 minutes.
If using chicken thighs, cut them in half. For a chicken breast, cut each piece in half.
Mix the coconut milk with all the ingredients in a large bowl, then add in the chicken and mix well.
This dish is so much nicer if the marination is made a day ahead. (If doing the marination overnight, do not add the vegetables).

Place the chicken mix along with the potatoes and carrots in a large oven dish.
Bake for 45 minutes in the preheated oven.

ROASTED PORK LOIN WITH PINEAPPLE PUREE AND ROASTED CASHEW NUTS

Serves 6

Ingredients

2kg pork loin
3tbsp sea salt flakes
2tbsp oil
6 cloves of garlic
4 star anise
6 sprigs of thyme
2 white onions cut in half
500ml Bulmer's or any cider
200g roasted cashew nuts
Pepper and salt

Method

Preheat the oven at 180°C for 10 minutes.
Score the skin of the pork belly with a sharp knife.
If there is time, rub the sea salt on the pork skin two hours before cooking and leave it in the fridge.
Pour the cider into a large oven dish, then add the thyme, garlic, star anise, and onions.
Place the pork loin on the dish with the skin side up and drizzle some oil.

Place the pork in the oven and bake for 20 minutes to get the skin crisp, then reduce the temperature down to 160°C and cook for further one and a half hours. By this time, it should have nice crackling skin. If not, increase the temperature back up and cook for a further 10 minutes.

Pineapple puree
1 large pineapple
1tsp dry chilli flakes
50ml apple cider vinegar
100ml juice from the tray

Method
Peel the skin of the pineapple and dice it into cubes taking out the hard centre.
Strain the liquid from the tray that the pork was cooked in and take 100ml.
Place all ingredients in a saucepan and cook till the pineapple is soft.
Pour it into a food processor and blend till smooth.
Let the pork rest for 15 minutes before slicing thinly.
Serve with the pineapple puree and scatter the roasted cashew nuts just before serving.

CHICKEN PILAF

Serves 6

Ingredients

250g basmati rice
500ml chicken stock
1tsp turmeric
2tsp salt
1tsp garam masala
3 chicken breasts diced or 4 chicken thighs
2 onions chopped.
10 peppercorns
5 cardamoms
1 stick cinnamon
3 cloves garlic
100g green peas
100g butter
10 curry leaves (optional)

To decorate
200g roasted cashew nuts
100g raisins
4 hard boiled eggs

Method

Marinate the diced chicken in garam masala and salt.
If using chicken thighs, remove the skin and cut each piece in two.
Heat a large saucepan and a tiny bit of oil first before adding the butter.
Once the butter melts, add the onions, garlic, curry leaves, peppercorns, cardamom and cinnamon stick. Sauté the spices well.
Mix in the chicken and seal the meat. Next add turmeric.
Rinse the rice once under the cold water tap, then mix it in with the other ingredients.
Pour in the chicken stock and reduce the temperature to medium to low before covering with a lid.
Let the rice and chicken cook for about 20 minutes.
Once the chicken and rice are cooked, mix in the peas and raisins.

Boiling the eggs
Place the eggs in the saucepan and add enough cold water to cover. Mix in a teaspoon of salt. Once the water starts to boil, time it precisely for 10 minutes to get a perfect boiled egg.
Once the 10 minutes pass, drain the hot water and add cold water to stop the eggs from discolouring.
Peel and cut in halves.
Put the rice into a dish and decorate with the eggs and roasted cashew nuts on top.
Serve with the mint sambol.

MINT SAMBOL

Serves 6

Ingredients
60 leaves of fresh mint
2 deseeded green chillies
100g fresh grated coconut
2 cloves garlic
Juice of 1 lime and salt

Method
Wash the mint leaves well along with the tender stems.
Place all ingredients in a food processor.
Add in the lime juice and salt.
Blend till smooth.
Serve with different Asian rice and Indian rice dishes.

SEABASS FILLETS WITH AUBERGINE AND GREEN BEANS

Serves 6

Ingredients
6 seabass fillets
100g green beans
1 aubergine
2tsp paprika
1tsp harissa paste
4tbsp oil
1 lemon
2tsp sea salt
100g parma ham

Method
Marinate the seabass fillets with lemon juice, paprika and sea salt.
Slice the aubergines very thinly lengthwise and rub on the harissa paste and salt.
Trim the green beans, and add to boiling water for 3 minutes. Drain the water and set it aside.
Heat a pan with the oil and cook the aubergine slice on one side, then turn over till lightly brown in colour. Take the aubergine slice of the pan and cook the seabass fillets skin side first. Once crisp, turn over and cook for about 12 minutes, depending on the size of the fillets.

Once seabass fillets are cooked, assemble on six individual plates or one large platter.
Place the aubergine slices first, then the seabass fillets and green beans.
Garnish with slices of parma ham.

SLOW ROASTED LAMB LEG WITH HARISSA PASTE

I dedicate this recipe to my dad. Growing up, I knew I could get away with anything if my dad was around. He is a very different character from my mum

Even if my food was barely edible when I was experimenting with cooking at a young age, he never criticised it and ate it most of the time and gave his advice later where things could have gone wrong. It still makes me smile when I remember my early days of cooking when I was around ten.

Whenever dad visited us in Ireland, he loved lamb and always loved any dish I cooked.

Sometimes when dad visits my sisters, he would mention my culinary skills, and the girls always call me back to tell me this.

Serves 6

Ingredients
3kg lamb leg
6 cloves of garlic
3tsp harissa paste
300ml red wine
6 sprigs of rosemary
2tbsp olive oil
Salt and black pepper

Method

Blend the garlic, harissa, salt and pepper to a paste.
Rub it onto the lamb leg.
Then pour the wine on top and leave in the fridge overnight.
The next day, put the rosemary sticks onto the tray.
Preheat the oven to 160°C for 10 minutes.
Then cook at this temperature for about three hours.
When cooked slowly for a longer time, the meat is tender and yet lovely and moist.

MONKFISH, ROSEMARY & BACON SKEWERS

Serves 6

Ingredients
1kg monkfish fillets
10 fresh rosemary stems (can also use bamboo skewers)
3tbsp olive oil
1tbsp garlic oil or 1 clove of fresh garlic
Juice of 1 lemon
6 bacon rashers
Salt and pepper to taste

Method
Cut monkfish fillets into bite-size pieces.
To prepare the rosemary skewers, strip the leaves off the stems leaving only a few at the end.
For the marinade, mix garlic oil, olive oil, pepper, lemon juice and salt in a large bowl.
Toss in the monkfish and leave it overnight or for at least two hours in the refrigerator.
Cut the rashers in half.
Wrap each piece of monkfish in bacon rasher.
Thread four monkfish pieces on the prepared skewers.
If not using rosemary skewers, chop some fresh rosemary and add it into the dish to get the flavour profile.
Cook in a preheated oven at 170°C for 20 minutes.

LENTIL CURRY

This recipe is for my wonderful and most precious son Dineth.

It's the first Sri Lankan dish he tasted, and he still loves the taste. It was first introduced to him by my mum.

Dineth certainly came into our world to make life more beautiful.

So, this is a recipe full of love.

Serves 6

Ingredients
200g red split lentils
500ml cold water
1 shallot finely chopped
200g washed baby spinach
1tsp turmeric
1tsp chilli powder
2tsp mild curry powder
200ml coconut milk
10 curry leaves

Method

Wash the lentils once or twice in cold water.

Place them in a saucepan and add all the ingredients except coconut milk, spinach and salt.

Pour 500ml of cold water and start cooking on medium heat.

In about 6 minutes the lentils will start changing colour and become tender.

Pour in the coconut milk and bring to a boil.

Take it off the heat and mix the spinach leaves, making sure that the leaves do not discolour.

Finally season with salt.

BAKED MACKEREL WITH PINE NUTS AND CHICKPEA STUFFING

Serves 6

Ingredients
6 whole mackerel cleaned
1 onion finely chopped
200g breadcrumbs
100g chickpeas
100g pine nuts
2tbs chopped dill
200g fresh asparagus
100g butter
4tbs olive oil
1tsp lemon zest
Juice of 1 lemon
Salt and pepper to taste

Method
For the stuffing
Melt the butter in a heavy-based saucepan.
Add the onion and cook till it's soft.
Drain all liquid off the chickpeas.
Put in the breadcrumbs, chickpeas, pine nuts, dill, and lemon zest.
Season with pepper and salt.
Take the head off the mackerel and clean the cavity and wash.

Marinate the mackerel with lemon juice, salt and pepper.
Using a sharp knife, make diagonal slashes along each fish.
Press the stuffing mixture to the cavity of the fish and transfer it to the baking dish.
Drizzle over with the remaining oil.

Preheat the oven at 180°C for 10 minutes and bake for 35 minutes.

To serve
Heat a pan with a bit of oil and cook the asparagus tips.
Season with lemon zest, pepper, and salt.

STEAK FILLETS WITH RED WINE JUS AND SAUTÉED KALE

Serves 6

Ingredients
500g fillet steak
1kg kale
4 cloves garlic
100g pancetta
4tbsp olive oil
Pepper and sea salt

For the jus
500ml red wine
100ml red wine vinegar
2 sprigs of rosemary

Method
Add two tablespoons of oil into an ovenproof pan.
Season the fillet with pepper and salt and seal all sides of the fillet in a hot pan.
Preheat the oven at 170°C for 10 minutes, then place the pan in the oven and cook for ten minutes for medium-rare. It can be cooked longer for your liking.
Once out of the oven, let it rest for 5 minutes.

For the jus
Place the wine, red wine vinegar and rosemary in a pan.
Let it reduce to half quantity, and the consistency thickening.
Once it has reduced in half, strain the jus.

For sautéed kale
Wash the kale and remove any hard stalks.
Heat a pan with the remaining oil and add in the pancetta. When the pancetta is golden brown and crisp, take it out of the pan.
Add the chopped garlic to the same pan and the washed kale. Cook till the kale is wilted and the colour remaining.
Take the kale from the pan to prevent it from further cooking. Mix in the pancetta.

When serving, add the kale first onto the plate, then cut the fillet to the appropriate size and place on top of the kale. Finally pour jus on the side of the plate.

CRAB MEAT, ANCHOVIES AND LINGUINE

Serves 6

Ingredient
500g dried fresh linguine
4tblsp olive oil
4 cloves garlic finely chopped
1 deseeded chilli
4 anchovies chopped
200g cherry tomato
1 lemon
150ml white wine
350g crab meat
Handful of chopped parsley
Salt to taste

Method
Cooking the linguine
Add about 4 litres of water to a large pot with a teaspoon of salt and bring to a boil.
Add in the linguine. For dry linguine, allow 10 minutes cooking time in boiling water but for fresh linguine, allow 6 minutes.

In a large saucepan heat, the oil, then add garlic, chilli and sauté. Keep it on medium heat and add the tomatoes, then increase the temperature and add the wine.

Bring it to the boil and add in the crab meat and anchovies. When the linguine is cooked, remove it from the water using tongs or a spaghetti spoon and directly add to the crab mixture. Gently toss the pasta, add the parsley, and serve straight away.

Note: If the pasta is not used straight away, drain the pasta and run under a cold water tap making sure it is not sticky.

ROASTED BUTTERNUT SQUASH AND BUTTER BEAN BURGERS

Serves 6

Ingredients
400g butter bean tin
3tbsp oil
2 medium size butternut squash
200g roasted cashew nuts
2tsp cumin powder
2 deseeded chillies
2 cloves of garlic
Handful of fresh coriander
1 red onion
100g breadcrumbs
Zest of 1 lime

Method
Preheat the oven at 170°C for 10 minutes.
Peel and deseed the butternut squash and cut into pieces.
Put them onto a baking tray, drizzle with oil and sprinkle sea salt flakes. Bake for 25 minutes.
Drain the butter beans and put them into a large bowl.
Chop the coriander, peel, and finely dice the red onion and add to the bowl with the beans.
Then chop the garlic and chillies finely and mix in with the rest of the ingredients.

Add in the breadcrumbs and cumin powder.

Place the cashew nuts in a food processor and chop them coarsely and add them to the mix.

Once the butternut is roasted, mash everything together with a potato masher.

Finely season with salt and the zest of the lime.

Shape into burger-shaped patties.

Line a baking tray with baking parchment, place the burgers in the tray, and bake for a further 15 minutes in the preheated oven.

PRAWNS IN COCONUT MILK

My sisters have always been there for me and encouraged me to pursue my dreams.

When we were growing up, my older sister Buddthika who didn't have the slightest interest in cooking, did interfere with a few of my dishes. We still laugh at these things.

Both of my sisters Dilini and Buddthika are my biggest fans.

There are no words to express my love for you and to express how important it is to have you both in my life.

This recipe is for both of you. We all loved this dish growing up living so close to the sea.

Serves 6

Ingredients

24 peeled and clean fresh prawns
2tsp chilli powder
1tsp coriander powder
1tsp mild curry powder
1 large onion sliced.
4 cloves crushed garlic
½ tsp turmeric powder
1 lemongrass
10 curry leaves
1 stick cinnamon
2tbs vegetable oil
200ml coconut milk

Juice of 1 lime
Salt to taste

Method

Marinate the prawns in lime juice and salt for one hour.
Cut the lemongrass into six pieces.
Add the oil onto a pan and sauté the onions, garlic, lemongrass, and curry leaves.
Mix in all the spices, add the prawns and mix to make sure all the spices have coated the prawns.
Reduce the temperature to a medium setting and pour in the coconut milk.
Cook for 10 minutes till the curry is reduced in volume. Taste and season with salt.

COCONUT SALAD (SAMBAL)

This is a recipe that I have dedicated to my lovely friend Debbie. She has always been very enthusiastic about Sri Lankan dishes, and this is a dish she really enjoys.

Through the years, she has supported me in many ways, and I really appreciate our friendship.

Serves 6

Ingredients
500g freshly grated coconut
100g diced shallots
1 clove of garlic
2 green chillies deseeded
50g dried chillies
1tsp chilli powder
1tsp salt
Juice of 1 lemon

Method
This is a straightforward simple recipe to accompany any rice dishes.
Peel and dice the shallots and peel and cut the garlic clove in half.
Place all ingredients in a food processor, squeeze in the lemon juice and mix it for 2 minutes.
Serve with plain white rice.

LAMB RACK WITH PARSLEY PUREE AND RED CABBAGE

Serves 6

Ingredients
2 lamb racks (6 portions per rack)
2tsp black pepper
100ml red wine
Sea salt flakes
2tblsp oil

Method
Marinate the lamb with all the above ingredients, if possible, the evening before.
Heat a pan with the oil and seal, and colour the lamb.
Preheat the oven at 170°C
Place in a baking tray and cook for a further 20 minutes to be medium to well done.

For parsley puree
200g washed and clean parsley leaves
100g fresh basil
2 cloves of peeled garlic
1tsp sea salt

Method
Place all ingredients in a food processor and blend till smooth.
Pour into a pot and gently heat just before serving.

Red cabbage
200g shredded red cabbage
1 star anise
100ml red wine
50ml balsamic vinegar
Salt to taste

Method
Add the red cabbage to a large saucepan.
Pour the red wine and balsamic vinegar on top.
Add in the star anise and salt.
Cook till the cabbage is nicely soft.

When serving, slice the lamb rack or leave it whole.

FISH MASALA

Serves 6

Ingredients
6 seabass fillets
2 white onions chopped
4 large tomatoes chopped
1tbs coriander powder
2tsp chillies powder
½ tsp turmeric powder
1tsp garam masala powder
150ml water
4tsb oil
To make the paste
2 green chillies
5 cloves garlic
2tbs ginger
Salt and black pepper to taste
Juice of 1 lime

Method

Wash the fish and marinate with lime juice, pepper, and salt.
To make the paste, place all ingredients in a food processor and blend till smooth.
Shallow fry the fish till it is crisp and golden brown in colour.
Reduce the extra oil into a separate pan.
And in the same pan that the fish was cooked, fry the onions and add in the paste.
Next, add all the spices, 150ml of water, and tomato and reduce it for a few minutes.
Then place the fish on the sauce, reduce the temperature and cook for an additional 15 minutes.

ROAST DUCK WITH POTATO PANCAKE AND SPINACH

Serves 6

Ingredients
6 duck breasts
Pepper and salt to taste

For the sauce
100ml apple cider
200ml apple juice
200ml chicken stock
4 sprigs thyme
1 stick celery
1 white onion

Method
For the sauce
Cut up the onion into large cubes.
Add all the ingredients and simmer until reduced in half.
Drain the contents of the pan with a sieve.
Reduce for a further 5 minutes.

For the potato pancakes
500g potatoes
2tsp salt
200ml milk
100g plain flour
4 eggs
Handful of chopped parsley
Pepper and salt

Method

Wash and peel the potatoes. Cut into cubes.
Place in a saucepan with the salt, cover with water and cook them.
Once cooked, drain all the water and place in a food processor and puree. (Do not over blend the potatoes or the texture would become gluey).
Let the potatoes cool down completely.
Mix the flour, eggs, milk, and fold in the potato mixture in a large mixing bowl.
Add in the parsley and salt.
Heat a non-stick pan with a bit of oil, add a ladle of the mixture. Reduce the temperature to low and cover with a lid while cooking.
Cook on one side till golden brown before flipping over to cook the other side.

For the spinach
Wash the fresh spinach.
Heat a pan, add some oil and mix in the spinach.
Once the leaves have wilted, drain all the excess liquid and season the spinach with salt and pepper.

For the duck
Season the duck with pepper and salt. Heat a frying pan and place the skin side down and cook till golden brown in colour. Preheat the oven at 180°C for 10 minutes. Place the duck in a baking tray skin side up and bake for 12 minutes. Let it rest in a warm place for 5 minutes before slicing.
To assemble, place the spinach first, then the pancake and sliced duck breast on top. Drizzle the sauce around.

STEAM FISH WITH GINGER

Serves 6

Ingredients
6 fillets of fish (preferably sea bass or trout)
2tsp chopped ginger
Pepper and salt to taste
Juice and zest of 1 lemon
6 pieces of banana leaves
6 bamboo skewers or toothpicks
6 9 inch squares of baking parchment and foil for wrapping

Method
Marinate the fish with ginger, lemon juice, zest and season with salt and pepper.
If using banana leaves, lightly heat the leaf on an electric hob, so there is the flexibility to fold.
Then wrap each piece of fish in the banana leaf and secure it with a skewer or toothpick.
If using baking parchment and foil, skewers are not required.
If you are using an electrical steamer or a regular pot, wait till the steam starts, then place the fish in the steamer. Cover with the lid and time for 20 minutes.

For the sauce
50g ginger
1 bunch of scallions
100g wild mushrooms
50ml soya sauce
50ml oyster sauce
6 cloves of garlic
2tblsp sesame oil

Method

Heat a pan with the oil add in the ginger and garlic. Sauté well.
Add in the sauces and let the mixture reduce a bit.
Add in the chopped mushrooms.
When the fish is cooked, place it on the serving dishes and pour the sauce on top.
Sprinkle the scallions before serving.

NOTES

BASIC CURRY POWDER BLEND

Serves 6

Ingredients
100g coriander seeds
90g cumin seeds
15 curry leaves
1 cinnamon stick
1tsp turmeric powder
12 cardamom pods
6 cloves

Method
Preheat the oven for 10 minutes at 170°C
Spread all the ingredients except turmeric powder in a baking tray.
Roast the spice in the oven for about 5 minutes. Place another tray on top so that the spices do not get blown away if using a fan oven.
While the spices are still warm, use a coffee grinder to grind all the spices. Next add the turmeric and mix well.
Store in an airtight container when cool.

NOTES

NOTES

NOTES